A WOMBAT in my DRAWER

AFFIRM press

Published by Affirm Press in 2016
28 Thistlethwaite Street, South Melbourne, VIC 3205.
www.affirmpress.com.au

National Library of Australia Cataloguing-in-Publication entry available for this title.
Title: A Wombat in my Drawer/ Ros Almond, author.
ISBN: 9781925344516 (paperback)

Cover and book design by Karen Wallis
Cover image © Australian Reptile Park and Devil Ark. Thanks to Amanda Woodbine.

Printed in China by 1010 Printing.

A WOMBAT

in my DRAWER

... AND OTHER AMAZING AUSTRALIAN ANIMAL STORIES

Ros Almond

INTRODUCTION

Australia is famous for a lot of things – incredible landscapes, beautiful beaches, friendly people and weird slang words – but nothing says 'Aussie' quite like our animals. From Skippy the kangaroo, to Dundee and his crocodiles, to the ridiculous number of deadly creatures we have to deal with, when the rest of the world thinks 'down under', they think animals.

So who'd have thought our animals could be even funnier, crazier, sillier and cuter than any of us realised? Every day there are adorable native critters getting into scrapes, pets going on wild adventures and farm animals making unusual friends. There are also some amazing humans working hard to look after our animals and ensure the best possible future for our wildlife and our environment.

In celebration of all our fascinating creatures, we've collected some of the very best animal tales from across the country.

We hope you enjoy reading it as much as we enjoyed creating it.

tinder

Pat, 30

SWIPE RIGHT, FOR SURE

Patrick the wombat is single and looking for love. Common wombats generally live alone in their burrows, but that doesn't mean they don't get lonely sometimes. After thirty years of bachelor life in Ballarat Wildlife Park, Patrick knows that he's getting on in years, and he's ready to settle down.

But finding a partner in life isn't always easy. Patrick isn't the most assertive wombat at the disco, and when it comes to the ladies he tends to get muscled out by the competition. Male wombats have to be quite aggressive to catch the attention of a mate, and Patrick, being a rather sensitive and sophisticated fellow, isn't one to get into a scuffle for the sake of a date.

So now he's taken the search online. According to the park's owner, Julia Leonard, 'He's after someone who enjoys late nights, especially dusk and dawn, can dig a good hole and enjoys feeding him carrots.'

Patrick's impressive age makes him (as far as we know) the oldest living common wombat in the world, and terribly worried about being too old for romance: Geoffrey Edelsten keeps managing to score with the younger ladies, so this dignified fellow is feeling confident that his impressive status as 'oldest living wombat' has him in with a chance.

Since Patrick has amassed more than fifty thousand Facebook friends, the crew at the Ballarat Wildlife Park decided to help him out and create a wombat Tinder profile to extend his search for the perfect partner. If you're trying your luck in the Ballarat region, keep an eye out for this buck-toothed gentleman burrowing his way onto your Tinder feed. 🐗

he also happens to be one of the largest, which is nothing to sniff at. He's already beating the average age of wombats in captivity by about ten years and those in the wild by around fifteen. Despite this, Patrick's not

Kangaroos may well be the go-to Australian mascot, but there's one underrated marsupial that we think could well rival the roo for athletic skill (and general awesomeness) and it's the humble wombat. These stocky little guys may look slow and steady, but that cute waddle hides an ability to run at a full speed of up to 40 kilometres per hour. To put that in perspective, the human footspeed world record is 44.64 kilometres per hour, so if you were to race a wombat over 100 metres there's a good chance you'd lose (unless you're Usain Bolt, of course).

But the cool qualities of the wombat don't end there: these guys are built to be the perfect digging machine. They create huge underground systems of tunnels and chambers, and if they need to escape down their burrows to avoid danger, they've got hard bums that are so tough few predators can get past them. And it gets even more impressive, because if a predator tries to crawl over the top of the wombat, it will give one big, powerful push and crush the silly intruder against the top of the burrow. In other words, don't mess with a wombat.

SMUDGE, the SUGAR GLIDER

Little Smudge the sugar glider was saved by an animal rescue organisation when he was a tiny joey. At the time he was a bit of a sad mess, weighing only 32 grams. A well-meaning person had spotted the sweet creature and thought they'd adopt him, but without the right knowledge and care, it's quite difficult to ensure the survival of baby native animals – especially ones as small as Smudge.

Sugar gliders generally stay in their mother's pouch for about ten weeks, but they aren't completely independent until they are between seven and ten months old. They're not really able to survive on their own without proper nutrients and care for quite some time. Luckily for Smudge, WIRES took in the little guy and he received the necessary intensive care. After two and a half months, Smudge was a lot stronger and was able to be released into the wild, joining a group of older sugar gliders. Although they're unbelievably adorable, these creatures are pretty fragile, so it's best to leave their care to the experts.

CRABBY CROWDS

Christmas Island isn't quite what you might expect – you won't find many presents or formal lunches there. Two-thirds of the island is a national park, home to many unique animals and plants. Admittedly, there are no reindeers, but you may see an interesting red creature or two … *million.*

One of the most incredible things about Christmas Island is the forest-to-coast migration of the tens of millions of red crabs that live there. This is, obviously, a whole lot of crabs. At the beginning of the wet season, they head to the water to spawn. Once they reach the shore, the males dig a cosy, romantic burrow before they're joined by their lady crab friends. After a nice evening together, the males go for a swim and then head back to the forest. The ladies produce eggs three days after their rendezvous, and then hang around the burrow for twelve or thirteen days while they get ready for the tide to rise.

The sea water eventually reaches the burrows and hits the eggs, then the baby crabs hatch and are washed out to sea. They cruise about in the water for a month or so, developing through various stages until they gradually make it back to shore. The tiny crustaceans then scuttle into the forest until it's their turn to return to the beach.

These crabs are well looked after. Parks Australia employees on the island have amazing strategies in place to protect the crabs from cars and humans during their migration. But the crabs do have one enemy that Parks Australia can't help them with: the yellow crazy ant. (That's not a lie, it's what they're called.) These ants shoot acid into the crabs' eyes (still true), which can be fatal to the crabs. It's like a comic book: a tiny, acid-shooting demon ant with 'crazy' in its name is the arch-nemesis of the smiley Christmas-y crab. We know who we're barracking for. 🦀

LITTLE DEVILS

Young Tasmanian devils may be sweet-looking creatures, but they wouldn't make the most pleasant dinner guests. These stocky little carnivores like to chill out during the day and scavenge for food at night, and they eat absolutely everything they find – bones, fur, the whole shebang. It's gross, but at least they leave minimal clean-up.

Tassie devils almost became extinct during the early 20th century when farmers who were determined to protect their livestock attempted to eradicate the scavengers. (Actually, Tasmanian devils are far more into leftovers than fresh kills and very rarely take their own prey. The livestock was killed by feral cats and foxes.)

Luckily devil numbers have grown since they became a protected species in 1941, but during the 1990s Devil Facial Tumour Disease (DFTD) was recognised as having a major impact on the population. To ensure the species' survival, a number of programs have been developed to try to find a cure for the disease, limit its spread and maintain healthy populations.

Devil Ark in Barrington Tops, New South Wales, plays an important role in a strategic breeding program of healthy devils to maintain a genetically diverse population. This adorable crew are part of that program. And while they're working that whole 'butter wouldn't melt in my mouth' look, you probably still shouldn't invite them to any fancy dinners.

did you know?

There's a push among some conservation and breeding programs to reintroduce Tasmanian devils to the mainland. They're one of the few Australian animals that could prey on young foxes and feral cats, which could help to limit these damaging populations. Choosing devils without DFTD would also increase the healthy population of the animals, but there's no way to predict what effect they could have on their new environment. The debate continues.

CUTE CHICK

In a story reminiscent of the literary classic _Are You My Mother?_ by PD Eastman, a tiny, adorable tawny frogmouth was blown out of its nest and went for a ride in a cherry picker to try to find its mum.

The chick, who was barely bigger than a 50-cent piece, was found by a local resident and taken to WIRES Northern Rivers, the local wildlife rescue organisation, where the little tacker was checked over and cared for until he was ready to be returned to the trees. But this was a bigger task than WIRES anticipated, since the nest was a fair bit higher than anyone could reach. It's good to have friends in high places, though; Steve Cubis, a local tree feller, offered his cherry picker to take the chick home.

WIRES was very impressed and grateful for the offer: 'Looking down from the basket I couldn't help but marvel at this enormous piece of machinery delivering such a tiny parcel such a small distance. How amazing that WIRES support is so strong from a non-member who took time and effort to deliver a service that we could not have managed without.'

In an ending that's enough to restore your faith in humanity, Steve found the nest, complete with the tawny's siblings and parents, and safely delivered the fluffball home.

did you know?

There are around fourteen related species of tree-kangaroo, two of which live in New Guinea. In Australia, along with the Lumholtz's tree-kangaroo, there's also the Bennett's tree-kangaroo. Both live in Queensland in pretty limited areas, and their ongoing survival depends on us preserving their natural environments.

is it a bird? no, it's a TREE-KANGAROO

Lucy the Lumholtz's tree-kangaroo is from the rainforests of the Atherton Tablelands, and like any member of her species she's a funny-looking little thing that seems to be about 50 per cent kangaroo and 50 per cent possum – but is 100 per cent gorgeous. Tree-kangaroos live in small groups, but generally like to keep to themselves.

Lucy was brought to a rescue centre in Queensland after she hopped into someone's house. Her vision isn't great, so if she was returned to the rainforest she could struggle to survive. Instead she lives quite happily at the Wildlife Habitat in Port Douglas, and has become pretty close to another Lumholtz's tree-kangaroo called Colin. They live together in the park, and they help to increase awareness of the potential vulnerability of these cute critters and the importance of preserving their limited natural environments to ensure their continuation as a species.

*The Phillip Island Penguin Foundation has more penguin jumpers than they could ever use, but they're still receiving jumpers today. To reiterate: please do not knit a penguin a jumper. Instead, we suggest that you donate to the Penguin Foundation to ensure that the high-quality care of these little penguins can continue.

PENGUINS in JUMPERS

In 2000, an oil spill off the south coast of Australia affected Phillip Island's little penguin population. The oil coated and matted the penguins' feathers so that the birds were unable to fluff up, dry off and keep warm.

The penguins' reaction was to try to preen their feathers, but since ingesting even a small amount of the oil could kill the birds, the preening had to be stopped. Eventually, the Phillip Island Penguin Foundation discovered a solution: covering the penguins' feathers with little woollen jumpers. Genius! Because it was such an adorable solution (and penguin jumpers don't take anywhere near as long to knit as human jumpers) the Foundation was soon swamped with tiny knitwear – far more than they could possibly need. The excess jumpers were used to dress toy penguins that were sold to raise funds for a new wildlife clinic. The hope is that the clinic's updated facilities, emerging cleaning technologies and the penguin jumpers, will all contribute to better outcomes in the event of another oil spill.

DUSTY the KANGAROO

Two-year-old Dusty's family isn't like most kangaroo families: it's made up of a mix of canines, humans and, of course, one little marsupial ... who thinks he's a dog.

Dusty joined the Stewart family after his mum was killed in a car accident. Luckily, Ashley and Felicity Stewart found him on the side of the road and decided to take him home. They fed him and took care of him, and over time the joey grew strong and happy in his new environment. Dusty's rescue shows how important it is to carefully check Australian marsupials after they've been involved in accidents with vehicles, because it might just be a mother with an orphaned joey. Most of the time these rescued animals are best taken to the nearest wildlife centre, but since a lot of places in Australia are too remote to have a centre nearby, occasionally these survivors become the responsibility of their rescuer.

These days, Dusty lives on the back verandah of his family home with Lilly the golden retriever and Rosie

RHINO-RACK
Sunseeker II

DIESEL

the border collie, who are more than happy to share their space with the new recruit. Dusty also joins the dogs in the back of the ute for drives around the property, and he tries to steal their treats. He loves pats and cuddles so much that it's easy to forget he's not a dog himself! While Dusty's free to explore the farm as he pleases, he always chooses to come back to his bed on the verandah. He also wears a reflective collar, because kangaroos are pretty quiet, so he can be very difficult to find at night.

Dusty has a special relationship with Lilly – in fact, Ashley reckons that Dusty thinks Lilly is his mum. He follows her around and gets a bit antsy if she's off on adventures without him. Dusty shows us that some young animals can adapt well to new lifestyles, as long as they're in safe and loving environments. If Dusty was returned to the wild now he would probably struggle, but there's no doubt he's doing rather nicely as part of the Stewart family.

BAZZ gets a BUZZ OUTTA BEEKEEPING

While working dogs are pretty common in Australia, they don't usually need to wear a uniform to get their job done. But Bazz's career is a bit different to that of the average working dog. The four-year-old Labrador lives with his owner, Josh, at an apiary in Tintinara, South Australia, and he's been specially trained to sniff out American foulbrood, a disease that wipes out bee larvae and messes with honey production.

Sniffer dogs are very helpful to humans (unless those humans have just got off a flight from Amsterdam), because their sense of smell is so strong they can detect odours that we can't even imagine. Labradors' damp noses, for example, have around 220 million olfactory receptors compared to the five million in a human nose. By sniffing rather than breathing regularly, dogs are able to direct odours straight into a specialised region of their brain. Each additional sniff adds up to trigger the dog's olfactory receptors and help it identify the scent. This all means that dogs smell much better than humans. (Wait a second ...)

Bazz is the first Australian dog to have been carefully trained to work in apiaries, and his incredibly perceptive sense of smell means that he's able to detect the disease early, before it destroys any larvae. It takes Bazz less than an hour to check the same number of beehives that five human apiarists need a whole three days to check. Clearly he is far better at this part of being a beekeeper than any human.

To smell whether or not the bees are infected, Bazz has to get pretty close to the hives – and at the start, the poor fella kept getting stung (bees are known to be pretty ungrateful). There are other apiary dogs just like Bazz sniffing out foulbrood in parts of the USA, but the winters are so cold and snowy there that the bees hibernate, allowing their four-legged protectors to do their jobs in peace. But there's not much snow in South Australia, so Josh designed a special suit for his canine co-worker – to protect him and also to give him that extra dash of style. Bazz took a while to get used to his new outfit, but with his suit on he can now do his job safely.

GOAT & KANGAROO BFFs

In Seaford Meadows in South Australia, it's said that you can find a certain mob of kangaroos with a rather unusual member. A large wild goat has struck up a long-term friendship with the roos, and the big inter-species family has remained inseparable. For a long time the locals had nothing beyond regular sightings and reports to confirm the existence of this interesting group – that is until real estate agent Naomi Will managed to capture a picture of the crew relaxing together in a grassy paddock.

Goats are herd animals, so naturally they prefer a bit of company, but generally they gravitate to friends that are more, well, goaty. Still, this rogue giant (who Naomi originally thought was a donkey) just goes to show that the family you choose can be just as important as the family you're born into. The goat's chosen herd of kangaroos might have a different way of doing things, but these open-minded animals are all happy to compromise and appreciate one another's unique qualities.

PUGGLE POWER

Leo the baby echidna was brought into the Healesville Sanctuary after being found, at only one month old, in a garden bed in Badger Creek, Victoria. When echidnas are babies (known as puggles) they don't have any of their characteristic spikes and can't even open their eyes, so while they're very cute, they also look a bit like they're made from PlayDoh covered in the skin of an earthworm. Leo was also tiny, weighing only 110 grams – about as much as a tomato. A little pink earthworm PlayDoh tomato? Absolutely adorable.

Echidnas, like platypuses, are a type of mammal called a 'monotreme'. They are laid in eggs, like reptiles, but are warm-blooded and drink milk, just like every other mammal. The milk is excreted by the mother through little pad openings on her stomach, which her babies can suck up with their strange mouths. Echidnas have snouts with long, sticky tongues that allow them to collect insects and worms. They don't have any teeth, so their strong tongues are important for helping them crush up food inside their mouths. It makes drinking an interesting procedure. Lisa and Kelly, two keepers at Healesville Sanctuary, had to feed Leo milk off the palms of their hands so that the puggle could drink it.

Echidna puggles are weaned when they're about seven months old, and they usually stay pretty close to their mums until they're about a year old. Because of this, Leo needed to be looked after for a while to make sure he would be strong enough to survive on his own.

Leo grew bigger and bigger every day, and soon started growing his fur and spines. He now looks less like a worm and more like the pinecone-y echidnas we know and love.

did you know?

Want a cool Aussie animal as a pet? There are a range of views on whether keeping native animals as pets is a good idea or not. On one hand, it means less culling, and it could help to preserve vulnerable populations. It would also minimise the number of damaging dogs and cats kept as pets. On the other hand, some of these animals struggle in domestic environments. They require additional care and a long-term commitment from owners. It's an interesting and important debate.

SUPERDOG and the ORPHANED JOEY

Dogs sometimes get a bad rap when it comes to their effect on native animals, to the point where they've been banned from Australian national parks to ensure the protection of the wildlife. Sometimes, though, dogs prove that they're capable of a lot more than instinctive aggression against our local fauna.

Rex, a German shorthaired pointer cross, performed a life-saving rescue mission after discovering a kangaroo that had been killed by a car near his home in Bells Beach. Rex became preoccupied with the kangaroo, and while his owner, Leonie Allan, was worried he'd found a snake, it turned out that Rex had found something less dangerous and much more adorable.

He'd sensed that something wasn't right and carefully rescued a little joey from its mother's pouch.

The ten-year-old pooch carried the four-month-old joey in his mouth so gently that it remained cool, calm and completely unharmed. The pair got along swimmingly and were soon cuddled up together.

Leonie took the joey to Jirrahlinga Wildlife Sanctuary, where he'll be looked after until he's old enough to live independently. Tehree Gordon, the owner of the sanctuary, is very impressed with Rex's efforts, noting that Rex was so gentle that the joey wasn't even distressed, which is pretty rare for such an interaction. Rex's actions show that good training can help dogs to tolerate the native animals with which they share their environments.

SIRI the CHEETAH CUB & IRIS the PUPPY

Siri isn't just adorable – she's also an important addition to the vulnerable coalition of cheetahs living at Taronga Zoo in Sydney. (There are some pretty odd collective nouns out there, but 'coalition' is up there with the weirdest.)

Cheetahs are incredible animals; they're the fastest land animal, capable of reaching speeds of up to 120 kilometres per hour, which is faster than you're allowed to drive in most Australian states. They're good at hunting, but they're not so good at defending themselves against predators. They're also not doing so great on the survival front at the moment: deadly threats to their habitat, competition for food and the illegal pet trade are having a significant impact on the wild population. Plus, while cheetah mums can have up to nine cubs at once, most of those in the wild don't survive until adulthood, and cheetahs don't breed well in captivity.

With so much at stake, the keepers at Taronga Zoo faced a tough problem when they realised that Siri's mum was showing signs that she would reject her cub. Usually cheetah litters contain three to five cubs, but Siri was born without a single sibling. In the wild, solo cubs are often abandoned because they have less chance of survival, but luckily Siri had the keepers on her side. They decided to do everything they could to make sure that Siri survived, and that she'd grow up to be healthy and socialised ... so they got her a puppy. Iris is a big, strong retriever–mastiff cross who can hold her own against the young cat. Siri sometimes seems less than impressed by her new companion, but luckily Iris is pretty oblivious.

While it would have been better if Siri could have been raised by her mum, a companion like Iris will help to ensure that she develops well and learns the essential natural social interactions that will allow her to thrive – plus she gets to be one half of an adorable pair.

CANE TOADS

So, cane toads are the worst.

They're a huge problem in parts of Australia, damaging native populations of plants and animals; in Kakadu, for example, the biggest threat to biodiversity is native animals consuming cane toads and dying from the poison. They were brought in to protect cane sugar plantations from native grey-backed cane beetles, but things got out of hand pretty quickly. Because they're introduced, they have no natural predator or parasite, and therefore they JUST DON'T DIE – except, you know, during cane toad cricket ... which we definitely do not condone.

Despite all this, there might be some value to the pervasive pests. Dr Jing Jing from the University of Queensland has found that cane toad poison has some amazing qualities, attacking some cancer cells while sparing healthy ones – in particular, it's been shown to be effective at killing prostate cancer cells. The researchers are trying to work out how to deliver the poison in a way that isn't dangerous to the rest of the body. They're hopeful that soon the unwanted intruders will redeem themselves with this life-saving surprise. Fingers crossed!

PEBBLE the JOEY

Pebble the kangaroo was rescued by Ballarat Wildlife Park after she became an orphan at seven months old.

Because she was too young to join the mob of kangaroos without her mum to help her out, she was adopted by Luke, one of the keepers at the wildlife park. The two became inseparable. She followed him around during the day and slept inside the house at night, even curling up in her makeshift pouch to watch *Border Security* in the evenings.

Sometimes it's not in a kangaroo's best interests to be released back into the wild after the animal has developed a close relationship with a human. At a lot of rescue parks, there's a mob of similarly raised roos that have a semi-wild, semi-tame lifestyle.

the TERRIBLE BBQ GUEST

Snakes are one of those dangerous animals that are used to prove that Australia is trying to kill its inhabitants. And yeah, there are a lot of snakes and many are venomous, but more Australians die each year being stung by bees than bitten by snakes.

So while it makes sense to be wary of things that can hurt you (like snakes, but also, you know, cars and bees), snakes aren't necessarily out to attack you – and sometimes, they're adorable and silly, like Winston the python.

Winston should be more careful about what he eats. His owner was feeding him his usual meal of rats (mmm) with a pair of barbecue tongs when the python gulped down the metal tongs instead.

Even though snakes can usually regurgitate their food whole, the tongs were just too big – they were about one-third the length of Winston's body and were pretty seriously stuck in his stomach. Dr Oliver Funnell, a vet at the University of Adelaide, had to perform surgery on the python to remove the implement. Happily, Winston the silly snake recovered, and hopefully he's learned a lesson about biting off more than he can chew.

CHIP the EMU HERDER

Chip the eight-year-old kelpie is a smart dog with a rather unusual job. Chip lives on a farm in Kerang, Victoria – an emu farm, in fact – and his work involves rounding up a flock of 2500 emus every day. He's such a natural with these intimidating birds that he can gather the huge flock much more quickly than his fellow farm workers, Jeff and Bev, can.

As well as being an Australian icon, emus are bred for their meat and their fat (which is turned into oil that's said to have therapeutic properties). Emu farms aren't very common in Australia at the moment, partly because they're quite expensive to establish, so Chip's job of protecting the emus and making sure they don't escape is a rare and important one.

Chip is very gentle with the emu chicks because he knows they're only babies. When the birds are bigger, though – much bigger than Chip himself – he's not afraid to boss them around. Sometimes the emus give him a painful peck but, ever the professional, Chip never responds with anger. He knows that patience and the ability to withstand such rude behaviour are key selection criteria for the role of emu-herder.

When it's not time for work, Chip also plays games with his flock of emus. He pokes his feet underneath the fence of the paddock for the big birds to try to peck. (Gee, fun game, Chip.)

Jeff says he's very grateful for Chip's help, and reckons that he's a really top dog.

SWINO
the WILD PIG

Swino, a wild pig from Port Hedland, Western Australia, was a big troublemaker. After stealing – and drinking – eighteen tinnies, Swino went on a drunken spree around a campsite. He knocked over tents, rummaged through rubbish and picked a fight with an innocent cow in a nearby paddock who was just minding her own business. After wreaking all this havoc, Swino passed out underneath a log next to a river to sleep it off. We've all been camping with that guy around, haven't we? So you can imagine the annoyance of Swino's fellow campers the following day.

Only a month after Swino brought the problematic drinking behaviour of wild pigs to the attention of the country, he was killed in a car accident in the Pilbara. He wasn't driving the vehicle, and it cannot be confirmed if alcohol was involved in his untimely demise. Hopefully Swino's story will act as a deterrent for other boozy pigs.

CUTEST COUPLE AWARD

Anzac the kangaroo joey and Peggy the wombat joey are adoptive siblings with a difference – and it's about as heart-melting as it gets. Both Anzac and Peggy's mums were killed after being hit by cars, but these little orphans were lucky enough to be saved by people who were careful to check the pouches for joeys.

Anzac was a few months old when he was rescued and brought to the Wild About Wildlife Rescue Centre in Kilmore, Victoria. Peggy had already been living at the shelter for a while, and because the young marsupials shared similar body movements and heartbeats, the staff at Wild About Wildlife thought it would be a good idea to pair them up. The adorable duo got along like a house on fire, and they even shared a pouch at bedtime.

While their different body shapes and sizes meant they couldn't share the pouch for long – Anzac grew bigger faster, since kangaroos are pretty big animals – having that closeness and comfort during the important months of their youth helped them grow healthy, strong and confident.

About a year later, Peggy was ready to be released back into her natural habitat (with the workers at Wild About Wildlife keeping an eye on her from a distance). Kangaroos mature a little slower than wombats, so Anzac needed more time before he could be released. But his early friendship with Peggy gave the cheeky, happy roo the best possible chance to grow and survive in the wild.

It's pretty hard for kangaroos to move backwards. Their big feet and heavy tail make them great at leaping forward, but totally unable to reverse. Apparently, the idea that they can only move forward is the reason that the kangaroo (and the emu, who suffers from a similar affliction) were chosen for the Australian coat of arms, which is accompanied by the motto 'Advance Australia'. Get it?

On average, male eastern grey kangaroos weigh in at around 50 to 65 kilograms and stand up to 2 metres tall. They live for between eight and twelve years in the wild. Wombats can grow to about a metre in length and weigh around 20 to 35 kilograms, and they usually live for about fifteen years.

QUOKKAS
your new favourite animal

The quokka could well be the cutest animal on the entire planet. These cat-sized marsupials are friendly and pretty laid-back, and they look like they have a permanent smile on their chubby little faces.

Quokkas live in Western Australia, mostly on Rottnest Island and Bald Island, where they have become a serious tourist drawcard. As there are no natural predators for them to deal with on these islands, they've managed to build up relatively healthy populations – populations with an amazing lack of fear when it comes to the humans that visit them. Lately they've been finding international fame by getting in on the selfie craze, sticking their grinning faces into other people's photos (these animals were born to rule the internet).

But before you start googling 'buy a quokka', keep in mind that they're not really pet material – on the rare occasions when these independent fellas get freaked out, they've been known to do some serious scratching

59

with their long, clawed feet. Journalist Kenneth Cook learned this the hard way when he tried to befriend a quokka by offering it a taste of his lunch, to which the quokka responded by falling into a dead faint. Mortified, and afraid that he'd poisoned the animal, Kenneth put the quokka into his backpack, hopped on his bike and peddled off in search of help. Unfortunately, the quokka started to revive and was not impressed by the undignified position it had been put into. It leapt out of the bag, scratching and screaming at Kenneth before latching on to his ear, until Kenneth peddled straight off a cliff and into the ocean. Luckily neither of them suffered any long-term harm. So, no, quokkas aren't all sweetness and fun, but they're not going to gore you if you don't give them a biscuit. (Note: don't give them biscuits – it's bad for their digestion.)

Despite their happy life on the islands, on the mainland quokkas are threatened by introduced species such as foxes and cats. Land clearing has also limited their habitat, and it's all come together to mean that quokkas are now considered a vulnerable species. So if we want to keep these cute little firecrackers around, it's important that we protect them – and remember to keep our lunches to ourselves.

did you know?

Quokkas open their mouths to pant when they're hot, which is part of what makes them look so smiley.

LULU the SUPER-ROO

Lulu the hand-reared kangaroo clearly learned a thing or two from watching reruns of *Skippy*. In 2003, Lulu's carer Len was hit by a falling branch and knocked unconscious.

Things could have been pretty dire for Len if it wasn't for his trusty sidekick, a ten-year-old western grey who'd been rescued by the family as a joey after an accident that killed her mother. Lulu knew something was wrong, so she began 'barking' to draw attention to the situation. ('Barking' is a nice way to describe the noise kangaroos make when they sense danger – a sound not unlike someone snoring. Charming, eh?) After about fifteen minutes of Lulu's strange behaviour, the rest of the family went to see what she was so upset about. After they found Lulu guarding an injured Len, he was rushed to hospital where he was treated and made a full recovery. Lulu was awarded the RSPCA Animal Valour Award in 2004, which we think is well deserved. Her bond with Len indicates a very special, trusting relationship and shows again that family is what you make it!

the GREAT EMU WAR

Emus are terrifying creatures. When it comes to Australian animals, most people are scared of snakes, spiders, sharks, dingoes and crocodiles – and that's all well and good, but surely we should be more concerned by the fact that one of our national emblems is basically a feathered dinosaur.

Emus are the second-largest bird in the world (after the ostrich), reaching heights of nearly two metres. Their legs are among the strongest of any animal, and while they can't fly, they can run incredibly fast (around 50 kilometres per hour). They'll attack you if you get too close to their chicks, they make really scary noises, their eyes will haunt your dreams and they can even swim – so there are few methods of escape if one's after you. They're also virtually bulletproof, as the Australian Army discovered in the 1930s after declaring war on a rogue emu population.

In 1932, some rowdy emus – and by some, I mean around twenty thousand – made the people in the central districts of Western Australia mighty uneasy. Taking over the town, wrecking fences, eating crops, picking fights at the pub: these emus needed to be shown who was boss. The population of Campion, Western Australia, included a large number of recently returned soldiers from World War I, and they knew just what would sort those pesky emus out: machine guns. The veterans had a chat to the Minister of Defence about their idea to combat the emus, and the minister eventually agreed to let the human army take on the emu army. This decision to kill a big flock of birds became an actual, official military operation, and the army could head into the operation happy in the thought that the emus' feathers could make a rather dashing addition to their dress hats.

The humans gave it a red-hot go. They smashed out around ten thousand rounds of ammo, but reports indicated that they had only killed around one thousand birds. Apparently the birds were smarter, faster and trickier to shoot than anticipated. They could move out of range and hide among trees before the soldiers could aim, but, more worryingly, even when they had clearly been hit by bullets they didn't seem to notice. After several attempts to eradicate the birds, the human army gave up. Yep, the emus had won. The leader of the mission, Major Meredith, said, 'If we had a military division with the bullet-carrying capacity of these birds, it would face any army in the world. They could face machine guns with the invulnerability of tanks.'

Emus: 1. Humans: 0.

AN ODD
LITTLE COMBO

Oddball the maremma is one special canine; in 2005, she was given the important task of protecting a whole island's worth of tiny penguins.

It all started because the little penguins on Middle Island, south of Warrnambool in Victoria, were under threat. Foxes were sneaking across to the island during low tide to feast on innocent penguins, and humans were visiting in increasing numbers and crushing the penguins' sandy burrows. In five years, the number of penguins on Middle Island had dropped from two hundred to around ten. A number of interventions were introduced to protect the penguin population, and while closing the island to the public solved the human problem, foxes don't tend to be quite so respectful of 'Do Not Enter' signs.

Maremmas are originally from Italy, where they were bred to protect flocks of sheep from any sneak wolf attacks. They're such skilled and disciplined protectors that they've also been trained to protect birds – though by 'birds', we're generally talking about nothing more exotic than chickens.

However, local organic egg farmer Allan Marsh, known as 'Swampy', realised that these dogs – particularly Oddball, his fox-deterring pooch – might be the solution to the Middle Island penguins' problem. Because Oddball had been so well trained, she was able to take her chook knowledge and, with a bit of imagination, apply it to the strange, formally dressed little birds that needed her help.

Oddball's new position worked a treat, and her success was enough to encourage the council to train up additional dogs, Eudy and Tula, to work on the island for the six months of the year that the penguins live there. Since the maremmas began guarding the penguins, not a single fox kill has been recorded, and the penguin population is back up to around 180.

SNAKES on a PLANE

In what sounds like the plot to a terrible movie (so, so very terrible), four baby pythons mysteriously went missing on a Qantas flight.

The twelve little snakes packed safely in the cargo hold had dwindled to only eight little snakes, and yet there was no clear sign of an escape. The plane was grounded and evacuated, but the escapees were nowhere to be found. At first, it was thought that they had been eaten by their siblings, but the remaining pythons – who were rather offended by the accusations – didn't weigh any more than they had before boarding the plane, so were cleared of cannibalism charges.

Not to worry you or anything, but those missing snakes were never found. We recommend taking extra care next time you get your hand luggage out of the overhead compartments ...

COCKATOOS PREFER BLONDES

A cockatoo in Queensland only likes people with long blonde hair (which is pretty judgemental for a bird with a pink Mohawk). Poya, the Major Mitchell's cocky, was not at all keen on Tom Patterson, the new zookeeper who was dropping by to feed her every day, and he started copping a bit of attitude from her – something that had never happened to any of Poya's previous (blonde, female) keepers.

Clearly something about the change of zookeepers was so upsetting to Poya that there was just no getting around it. After eight months of struggling with the temperamental bird, Tom began to wonder if his hairdo might be the problem. He jokingly tried on a blonde wig in an attempt to soothe the bird, and it seemed to do the trick – Poya found him much more to her taste. The other birds have also warmed more to Tom now that he's rocking his Gwyneth Paltrow do, so he's been donning the new look for every visit to the feathered fashion police.

SUDO & SIESTA

Siesta the donkey foal, who's only a little tacker because she was born two weeks early, is one of the cutest baby animals around. And she's made even cuter by the fact that her best friend is Sudo the dog.

Sudo treats Siesta like her own baby, despite the donkey being quite a bit larger than the average puppy. Sudo and Siesta's owner, donkey breeder Linda Jay, says that the two are as close as can be, and they even snuggle down and sleep together. Luckily Siesta's biological mum is an open-minded donkey and doesn't get jealous or overly protective of her foal. As Sudo has never been anything but gentle and affectionate with her young friend, it's clear Siesta's mum has nothing to worry about.

Donkeys and dogs both like living in packs and neither are particularly fussy about the species of that pack, so the two are more than happy to find that special friendship with each other.

KOALAS in MITTENS

While koalas are always cute – as is anything wearing mittens – the story behind these photos isn't all happy. Environments full of gum trees (the usual home for eucalyptus-loving koalas) are prone to bushfires, and the chilled-out marsupials regularly fall victim to these devastating natural disasters.

During bushfires, koalas often sustain burns to their paws, making it painful or even impossible for them to climb trees in order to feed, rest and sleep. Sore paws also make it painful for them to get away from predators.

After one such devastating bushfire, the International Fund for Animal Welfare (IFAW) put a call out for members of the public to sew and donate koala mittens made of soft cotton. These would help to protect the animals' paws while they healed. It's a gorgeous solution to a devastating issue, and has allowed the koalas to be returned safely and healthily to their native habitats.

Because of the appeal of this method of helping, IFAW were quickly inundated with a substantial number of koala mittens, and at the time of writing the organisation is not in need of any more. You can check the IFAW website for specific methods of helping out animals in times of emergency, but donations are always helpful and welcome.

did you know?

Koalas have fingerprints that look suspiciously similar to humans' fingerprints. They're so similar that it's practically impossible to tell the difference between a koala's prints and a person's. Weird, right? And kind of scary – just think how many unsolved burglaries could actually have been committed by koalas ...

'did you see frank? HE WAS PISSED as a PARROT!'

Since 2010, a weird illness has been hitting the lorikeet population of Darwin. A huge number of the parrots are stumbling around and crashing into things, or falling out of trees before passing out – basically being obnoxious drunks.

The sloshed birds were picked up off the side of the road and taken to wildlife centres and animal hospitals to recover from their hangovers. While this is kind of funny, it's a bit of a worry for the veterinary community – no one is totally clear on what's making the lorikeets act so toasted. For a while it was assumed to be fermented fruit, but more recenty it's thought to be a nasty seasonal virus. (A good excuse to keep in mind.) While no one enjoys a hangover, the birds can die from their benders because the illness affects their respiratory tracts. They are also much more likely to make poor decisions that leave them more vulnerable to predators (and more likely to pick fights with their mates and sing 'Khe Sahn' at karaoke).

SEALPRANO

A New Zealand fur seal has decided that he prefers the cultured life and has settled in on some steps at the Sydney Opera House. Despite all the action that takes place there, he's countered expectations and has lived at his new digs for about a year. The five-year-old youngster is happy and healthy, and there are enough fish in the harbour to keep him well fed. It's also the perfect spot to sunbake and belt out some arpeggios while digesting lunch.

It's not very common for seals to live so close to humans, but his comfort in the environment is thought to be a good sign and might encourage other seals to move to the area. Their movement to the mainland is also a good indication that the fur seal population is slowly but steadily recovering from its near extinction in the 1800s.

Everyone's on board with welcoming the new resident, and the steps have been blocked off to give the seal a little bit of privacy as he listens to the music from the opera house. He's generally a fan of classical music, but also enjoys the occasional stand-up comedy gig.

a WOMBAT in my DRAWER

Kenny the wombat was rescued as a joey after his mum was killed by a car. He was bruised, and his nose and paws had been damaged, but otherwise he was very lucky to have been protected in his mum's pouch during the accident.

The little joey was taken to the Australian Reptile Park in Somersby, New South Wales, and was bottle-fed by Tim Faulkner, the park's manager. The wildlife park workers actively encourage people to stop and check the pouches of injured wildlife and make sure that little ones like Kenny have the best chance at survival. They also ask people to take note of the local injured wildlife hotline numbers in the areas that they're driving through.

As Kenny grew up into a plump young wombat, he became more and more mischievous. While he still slept in a makeshift pouch indoors to keep warm and safe at night, like all teenagers he enjoyed pushing the boundaries, so he started exploring

different areas of the house in search of good spots to take a nap. He found somewhere especially warm and comfortable in his caretaker's bedroom: the clever joey learned how to nudge open the sock drawer to get to its soft and snuggly insides. He'd climb in (eventually – it'd take him a while because he was only little and not terribly coordinated) before making himself a hollow and falling fast asleep.

With all the rest he's getting, hopefully one day soon Kenny will be strong enough to return to the wild and live with other wombats, although he probably won't find such a comfortable bed again. Burrows have got nothin' on socks.

DONKEY GUARD

Dora the donkey and Diego the calf are best friends. Dingoes and feral dogs had repeatedly attacked and killed Majella Rayment's young calves, and she was becoming increasingly sad and frustrated. After losing about twelve of her poddies, Majella decided to hire the ultimate security guard: a baby donkey.

Donkeys are great 'guardian animals' that keep predators such as dingoes away. They really don't like dogs and are happy to take them on in a fight. Little Dora's been entrusted with taking care of her new friend Diego.

Majella bottle-reared the donkey, who now seems like quite a mature young jenny. She's very protective of Diego and gets worried when he's out of her sight, which is a good sign for Diego's survival. Majella can rest easy knowing her calf is in good hands (or, you know, hooves). Even though Dora is only close friends with one of the calves, her presence in the paddock is enough to protect the rest of the herd from dingo attacks. By far one of the best security guards going around.

EMBARRASSING DADS

Samson the poodle may look like the ultimate dag dad, but his surrogate kids don't seem to mind. He's an incredibly kind and lovely carer who's willing to foster any orphaned animal that comes his way.

He lives at the Jirrahlinga Sanctuary in Geelong, and he has helped to raise kangaroo and wombat joeys, as well as this litter of eleven dingo puppies. The curly-haired poodle – who looks very Craig McLachlan circa 1990 – takes it all in his stride and cares for his charges regardless of their species.

Despite appearing interminably silly, poodles are actually pretty awesome dogs. They're very intelligent but also keen to please, so they're capable of independent thought with the intention of helping out their owners. Their unique coats have only one layer of fur, which means they're hypoallergenic, and they have webbed feet so they're awesome at swimming: all things that add up to make Samson a wonderful dad.

The healthy, happy dingo puppies came from a conservation rescue facility in Victoria. Their time with Samson at Jirrahlinga is intended to help them to become socialised with humans and other animals, but while Samson is extremely well mannered, he probably won't pass all of his good training on to his adopted kids. Dingoes may be able to interbreed with our pet pups, but they are still a separate species to both wolves and domestic dogs, which means that they've got some pretty wild and aggressive instincts that are impossible to train out. Still, it is possible to influence their behaviour to a point, and the hope is that Samson will help to bridge the gap between these cute young pups and their human keepers.

did you know?

Dingoes are considered a pest in some parts of Australia, but in other parts they are a protected species. Their continuation as a species is threatened because of their ability to breed with other dogs, which dilutes their unique characteristics. This reinforces the need for feral dog populations to be contained. (So here's a friendly reminder to desex your dogs and avoid contributing to this issue.)

FRECKLES the CAT

Freckles the cat's 1000-kilometre adventure across New South Wales is a pretty impressive feat and an Australian record.

Freckles' family moved from Wagga Wagga to Muswellbrook, but it seemed Freckles wasn't too keen on that decision. So the independent-minded feline walked all the way back to Wagga.

Six months later, Freckles showed up at his old house – the distance he'd walked would take nearly seven hours by car. But Freckles was less than impressed to find strangers living in his house. So he turned around and headed back to Muswellbrook.

He didn't quite make it home and was taken to the Muswellbrook Animal Shelter where his microchip was scanned, his family were called, and the whole story began to fall into place.

Freckles wasn't in the best of health after his long journey, and sadly he passed away not long after being reunited with his family. But thanks to his amazing trek, the adventurous feline certainly won't be forgotten.

MANDY & MANDY to the RESCUE

Mandy the goat and Mandy the border collie might be an unlikely rescue team, but they worked together to save the life of their owner, a farmer (and presumably Barry Manilow fan) called Noel Osborne. 78-year-old Noel was working on his farm in Benalla when a cow knocked him into a cow pat – which isn't even the worst part of the story, because he also broke his hip. He couldn't move and there was no one around to hear him calling for help.

Noel may have been unoriginal in his choice of pet names, but Mandy and Mandy still did all that they could to help him through the ordeal: Mandy (the goat) let Noel drink her milk, which meant he stayed hydrated, and Mandy (the dog) stuck by Noel's side, keeping him warm overnight.

After a whole five days, some of Noel's friends stopped by to find him lying on the ground and called an ambulance. He wasn't in good shape, but he was still alive, which wouldn't have been the case without his animals. Mandy's a pretty handy animal to have around! And so is, uh, Mandy.

ESCAPEES

It seems that the orang-utans in our zoos saw all the fun our native animals were having and wanted to get involved! In 2015, two orang-utans in Australian zoos managed to escape their enclosures within two weeks.

Orang-utans are extremely smart, inquisitive and very good at getting around obstacles. But they're still unpredictable animals with enough strength to cause serious damage. So when Malu the Sumatran orang-utan got out of his enclosure at Melbourne Zoo, it sent the whole place into lockdown. It took an hour for the hairy escapee to be apprehended and returned to his enclosure.

Then two weeks later on the other side of the country, it was Teliti's turn to explore the world outside her Perth Zoo enclosure. The curious young ape managed to climb a shadecloth and jump out onto the boardwalk, mingling with her fans like a real celebrity. But it wasn't long before she decided that the human world wasn't all it was cracked up to be and returned, unharmed, to her enclosure.

MOCHA & RUSTY

Mocha the Hungarian vizsla–labrador cross and Rusty the grey appaloosa from Pimpinio in western Victoria have an odd but lovely friendship. Ever since Mocha was a pup, the pair have been rather fond of each other. In their younger days, the two best mates would muck around together as if their size difference was nothing: Rusty the horse happily let Mocha lick his eyes and eyelashes, and Mocha didn't mind Rusty chewing on her ears and neck – which sounds like a pretty creepy relationship, but both of them were okay with it.

The pair played chasey for hours on end, throwing in the odd 'wizzy-dizzy' when Rusty would pick Mocha up by her collar to lift her a little way off the ground. Even though Mocha would sometimes cheekily try to lure Rusty towards the electric fence and give her companion a bit of a shock, Rusty was always careful not to hurt his buddy. 'Mocha would let Rusty know on the occasions he did get too rough – she'd yell, "Rough!"' says their owner, Helen Coutts.

In 2013, Mocha got quite sick with toxoplasmosis, a disease spread through cat faeces. (Mocha would like to warn other dogs that while eating poo may seem like a harmless jaunt, it can have disastrous consequences that take a while to recover from.) Her illness significantly affected her balance, movement and confidence, and she became slightly apprehensive about playing with Rusty. Horses are great at interpreting body language, so Rusty took Mocha's changed behaviour in his stride, adapting to the new rules of their relationship. Their interactions became a lot more chilled out, and the pair began to take leisurely walks around the paddock instead of their usual high-intensity activities. Rusty's understanding helped Mocha get back to her old self, and that really is the kind of mate you want when you're going through a tough time.

HEATWAVE

In November 2014, an extreme heatwave in Casino, New South Wales, tragically caused the deaths of about five thousand black flying foxes, as well as a number of grey-headed flying foxes.

Because of the time of year, many of the bats were mothers with suckling pups, which made them particularly vulnerable to the severe weather. Incredibly, hundreds of the baby bats survived the heat, and wildlife volunteers searched the tragic scene to rescue these pups. The volunteers from WIRES gave the bats hydrating injections before transporting the babies to makeshift emergency hospitals. Because the little bats were still young enough to be carried by their mothers, they needed to be bottle-fed around the clock to ensure their survival.

Almost all of the pups managed to survive, which shows the positive impact that dedicated rescue teams like WIRES can have on native species and the ongoing importance of keeping these organisations well resourced.

ECHIDNA vs GUMBOOT,
gumboot wins

Echidnas are one of the oldest surviving species of mammal on the planet, so you'd think that they'd have developed heaps of innate wisdom to aid their survival and stop them from making dumb mistakes. But apparently that's not the case, and sometimes their decision-making leaves a bit to be desired.

Take, for example, this echidna who thought it was a good idea to have a snooze in a gumboot. The silly little guy was feeling worn out, and like any echidna, all he wanted was a nice warm burrow to nap in. And what cosier burrow could you find than an item of farming footwear? Getting into the thick, rubbery boot was easy, but because of his spikes and the limited space to perform a U-turn, the echidna was soon trapped. Echidnas' natural defence is to roll into a ball to protect themselves from stressful situations, but this strategy worked against him and only served to wedge him in further. Whoops!

Luckily, the gumboot's owner noticed that there was something awry with his footwear, and he took his spiky boot to the Ark Vet Hospital in Darwin. The vet was able to do some cobbling and free the animal from its rubbery prison, and fortunately the echidna was completely healthy after his ordeal – if a tad embarrassed.

did you know?

While echidnas have a lot in common with other mammals, it's their reptillian characteristics that (along with their fellow monotreme, the platypus) makes them special in the animal world. Echidnas have the lowest body temperature of any mammal, and they have a 'cloaca' (a single opening for reproduction, defecation and urination) like reptiles. Combine that with the fact that they lay eggs and their beaks have electro-receptors to detect their insect prey, and you've got one weird critter.

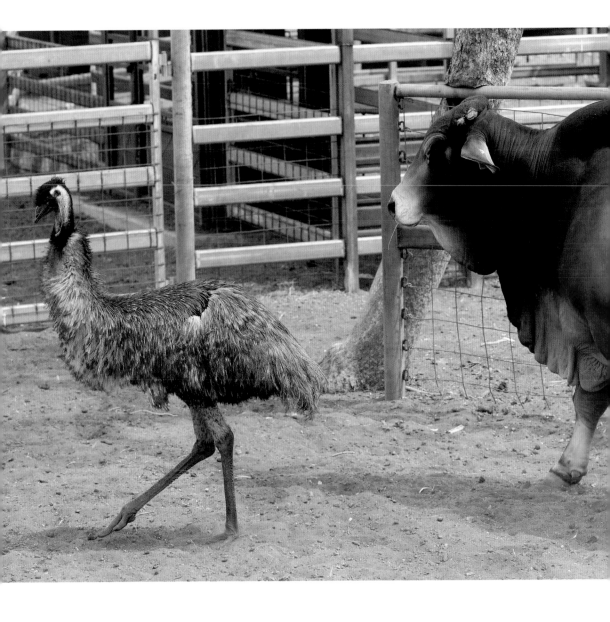

the EMU who thinks SHE'S a COW

Louie the emu was rescued in Aramac, Queensland, as a little chick, and she was raised alongside calves on grazier Margaret House's property. Since then, Louie's lived a happy life, but has never really got her head around the fact that she's an emu: the confused bird has always identified far more strongly with the cows she hangs out with, and considers herself a key player in the herd.

Louie's also formed a romantic attachment to Margaret's Brahman bull, and the pair spend most of their time together. Louie even likes to take a nap in the sun with her beloved. Unfortunately she's quite possessive, and her bullfriend isn't allowed near any of the cows – which has caused a bit of a problem for Margaret's herd. Louie isn't worried about that, though, because she's too busy trying to seduce the bull herself. Presumably she hasn't thought about the technicalities of such an interaction, or its implications, but it could be the beginning of an interesting new species ...

the EMU who thinks HE'S a HORSE

Emu the emu would much rather be a horse. About three years ago, when he was a rather young bird, he packed up and moved in with the Alice Springs police horses, and he liked horsing around so much that he decided to stick with the band. While Emu can come and go as he pleases, he's made his preferences very clear – mainly by strongly objecting to the many attempts that have been made to return him to a more typical environment.

Senior Sergeant Melinda Edwards reckons that Emu has 'taken on the equine lifestyle', and he eats and gallops with the horses. He's helpful when it comes to desensitising the horses, but less helpful when it comes to legitimate police business, and he doesn't realise that he isn't as valuable to the force as he believes. Two of the horses are accepting of the new recruit, but the other three are, according to Melinda, 'not so keen' on their two-legged counterpart. And none of them really appreciate the casual rump-pecking that Emu enjoys.

the EMUS who think THEY'RE PEOPLE

Emus generally aren't too keen on living with a lot of humans
– we're noisy and angry and always showing them nice food and
then shouting when they take a taste of it. But just like us, now
and then they feel the need for a change of scene – or, more
accurately, unlike for us, an ongoing drought causes food scarcity
for the wild population and forces the hungry birds into town.

In late 2013, around fifty emus waltzed into Longreach, Queensland, like they owned the place. While most of the residents were happy to welcome the visitors, the birds could be annoying: they refused to follow road rules and had no regard for the aesthetics of people's gardens. But because they're huge and somewhat terrifying birds,

they pretty much had free rein. The mayor, Joe Owens, acknowledged that they were causing 'a bit of a drama' but said that there's 'little you can do apart from physically driving them out of town, but then they would just turn around and come back tomorrow'. He concluded, 'We're just going to have to put up with them.'

CASTAWAY

Sophie Tucker is a pretty incredible dog with a pretty incredible story (and a pretty incredible name). In 2008, Sophie the blue heeler went for a boat trip with her human family, Jan and Dave Griffith. During their cruise the day started to turn dark; the wind picked up, and the waves got bigger and choppier. When Dave had his back turned to check something on the boat, Sophie fell over the side. The waves were so rough that Jan and Dave couldn't see where their poor hound had fallen, and they had to turn back to shore without her, devastated at losing their much-loved pet.

But Sophie wasn't keen on calling it a day. Amazingly, she somehow swam five nautical miles in shark-infested waters and made it to St Bees Island off the coast of Mackay. Even though dogs are good swimmers, it's pretty uncommon for one to last for more than half an hour in the water; they struggle to float, so they have to move constantly to keep their heads above water. The weather, too, was less than ideal, so it's an incredible feat that Sophie made it to shore. Not only that, but the well-cared-for pooch also managed to find water and food – and survive on the island for about five months. She certainly wasn't a favourite of the island's locals after she started honing her hunting skills on their baby goats.

Four months after their beloved pet's disappearance, Jan and Dave heard word that a dog fitting Sophie's description had been found on the island, so the next time the ranger's boat returned to the mainland, the Griffiths were waiting for it. Their hope was rewarded when they saw a worn out but very excited Sophie barking to them from on board the boat. Sophie returned to the comforts of domestic life quite happily, but her skills suggest that she'd be a real contender for a series of *Dog Survivor*. (Million-dollar idea, right?)

CASSOWARY RAMPAGES

While emus are undeniably scary, they've got nothin' on their colourful cousins, cassowaries. These prehistoric-looking birds have the weirdest headgear around and no qualms about kicking people, which makes them just a little concerning. (Really, though, they're only aggressive when protecting their eggs or chicks, when they're threatened or when they have become used to humans feeding them. Having said this, they are still related to dinosaurs, and dinosaurs are scary.)

Dennis Ward was in Cairns with his family checking out a wild cassowary from a 'safe' distance when the dino-bird started to look a bit ticked off. Dennis didn't take too long to realise that the cassowary was starting to get testy – shooting angry glares their way, putting its head down and making a strange booming sound that didn't bode well. Since Dennis didn't really want to be gutted by the giant bird's menacing middle toe (which is fair enough) he tried to make a hasty retreat. But the bird was quicker, and it took the opportunity to kick Dennis squarely in the back, sending him flying down a hill. Concerned onlookers called an ambulance, and luckily Dennis was okay. The smug bird headed back into the rainforest, content with its victory over its unwilling opponent.

There was another cassowary-related scuffle at the Visitor Information Centre at Mission Beach in Queensland. A female bird was far from impressed when the cassowary statue she was flirting with didn't respond to her advances. It just stood in place, staring at her. So she did what anyone would do in that situation: she kicked it a few times and broke its head off. Female cassowaries are strongly territorial and spend their forty-odd-year lifespan in the same area, so an unexpected encounter isn't generally met with friendship. The staff at the centre sensibly covered up the offending statue to avoid any further altercations.

WOMBAT
in a BEANIE

Plenty of kids (and adults for that matter) might dream of having a wombat for a pet, but Pinch the wombat proved that these stocky creatures can be as troublesome as they are lovable.

Pinch joined the Hume family after his mum was killed in a road accident. Alison and Eddy were going for a run at Dinner Plain in the Victorian high country when they came across a female wombat lying dead by the side of the Great Alpine Road, at a sharp corner known as 'Slippery Pinch'. Alison checked the wombat's pouch and found a joey lying safe and warm, so she wrapped him up and took him home.

Pinch spent his early days with the Humes lying bundled in a beanie sitting on top of a warm stove. As he grew, the little wombat started exploring the farmland around the family home, wandering through the bush at the bottom of their property. The family decided to let him live outdoors so he could get a taste of wild wombat life, but he was still a part of the clan (though he was also rather camera shy, and would often give the kids a nip when they tried to make him pose for family photos).

But as Pinch became more confident, he also got a lot cheekier: he liked to break into the house to steal dog food, leaving scratch marks all over the doors. One night, after yet another case of forced wombat entry, Eddy found himself chasing Pinch around the garden in the nude. The family decided it was finally time to help Pinch return to the wild for good, and the next morning they drove him up the road to let him free in the State Forest.

Many years later a senior wombat came to visit the Humes' back garden, but the old fella was unwell and died the next day. Ever since, the family has wondered whether it was Pinch coming home for one last visit.

KANGAROO PAWS

In January 2016, bushfires razed parts of Western Australia. While you could replace '2016' with any year and 'Western Australia' with most Australian states and this statement would still stand, the frequency of fires in Australia doesn't make them any less devastating to people or to the wildlife that are mostly left to face the flames unprotected.

Around Yarloop, vets from Waroona Veterinary Clinic were overwhelmed by the number of animals injured by the fire, and they worked around the clock to try to save the local wildlife. Some creatures were luckier than others – like this little guy, whose special socks will help his burned paws to heal so that he's able to be returned to the remaining bushland. This photo of the poor joey was so sad and sweet that it went viral and brought some much-needed attention to the work that vets do in fire-damaged areas. Waroona's staff treated all sorts of wildlife, pets and livestock in order to help them recover from burns and smoke inhalation, and over several weeks the patients were able to get better as they rested in the clinic and even in the vets' backyards!

Despite the enormous damage to homes and property in the area, the local community still donated cash and food to help out the Waroona vets as they worked. It just goes to show that people can be incredibly generous when it comes to taking care of animals, even during the toughest times.

a FISH out of WATER

Even though the koalas in Portland, Victoria, seem to enjoy living near the coast – you can hear them shouting, 'How's the serenity?' to one another on a breezy afternoon – they're not real beach bums. Koalas aren't quite made to swim: their heavy coats quickly become waterlogged, so it can be difficult for them to get out of rivers and swimming pools – and the sea.

The current of the ocean makes swimming a real challenge to poor, heavy koalas, and in 2008 the coast guards in Portland saved one lucky koala from drowning. By the time the guards realised that the furry creature in the distance wasn't just a dog having a dip, the not-quite-hydrodynamic marsupial wasn't breathing. The coast guards grabbed the soggy animal out of the ocean, drained the water out of him and performed CPR. They managed to resuscitate him and took him to the vet to be checked over. Luckily he was okay after his ordeal, but this very fortunate koala should probably stick to the boardwalk from now on.

DISCO SPIDER

Arachnaphobic? The solution to overcoming your fear might just lie in making the acquaintance of two of the prettiest, silliest spiders around. Known as 'sparklemuffin' and 'skeletorus' (no, we're not joking), these newly discovered species of peacock spiders live across various parts of eastern Australia. They're also very beautiful: sparklemuffin's male members have blue and red bodies that rival any outfit you might see at the Rainbow Serpent Festival, and skeletorus's black and white markings would help him to fit right in at a hip inner-city coffee shop.

Scientists have discovered fifty-seven species of peacock spider (*Malatus*) so far, almost all in Australia. They tend to live on the ground and in small bushes, and each has its own unique appearance. But something they all have in common is a seriously funky look and some next-level dancefloor skills to match.

These spiders are only around half a centimetre long, and they have dance moves like you wouldn't believe. When a male spider is looking to attract a mate, he raises his third set of legs and waves it in the air like he just don't care, then spreads out his abdomen, flapping and wiggling it about to impress his beloved.

These little multi-eyed, multi-legged creatures are excellent beyond description, so we urge you to put down this book right now and type 'peacock spider dance' into YouTube. Quick. Your day will immediately be better.

AN ECHIDNAPPING

While animals can be pretty weird sometimes, people can be even weirder. Especially when they do things like put on a mask, break into a wildlife sanctuary and kidnap a monotreme.

Poor Piggie the echidna had no idea what was coming when she was snatched from her home in Currumbin Wildlife Sanctuary. When her keepers arrived one morning to find her missing, the search began. But a few days later it seemed that the thieves had thought better of their crime, and Piggie was found safe in the sanctuary again, having been slipped under the fence. When the culprits were finally arrested, they admitted that it was all just a drunken prank. They'd broken in hoping to find a crocodile (because of course), but when their search had failed they'd taken Piggie instead.

Piggie's keepers reported that she'd been very stressed by the experience, and could have been in real danger if she'd been kept for much longer. Luckily she recovered from her ordeal, and a few months later gave birth to a very photogenic little puggle of her own!

PHOTO CREDITS

EMBARASSING DADS: Dingo Puppies at Jirrahlinga Koala and Wildlife Sanctuary © Alex Coppel / Newspix

FRECKLES THE CAT: Freckles the Cat © Australian Broadcasting Corporation Library Sales

MANDY & MANDY TO THE RESCUE: A Border Collie and a Goat © imageBROKER / Alamy

ESCAPEES: Orangutan Cute © apple2499/Shutterstock

MOCHA & RUSTY: All photographs © Helen Coutts

HEATWAVE: Pup with Dummy © Lib Ruytenberg, care of WIRES Northern Rivers

ECHIDNA VS GUMBOOT:
Page 104: Echidna in gumboot x-ray © The Ark Animal Hospital NT
Page 106–107: Echidna in Gumboot © Elise Derwin / Newspix

THE EMU WHO THINKS SHE'S A COW: Emu and Cow © Adam Head / Newspix

THE EMU WHO THINKS HE'S A HORSE: Emu and Horse in Conversation © Australian Broadcasting Corporation Library Sales

THE EMUS WHO THINK THEY'RE PEOPLE: Emus in Longreach © Outback Pics, www.outbackpics.com.au

CASTAWAY: Sophie the Dog © Daryl Wright / Newspix

CASSOWARY RAMPAGES:
Page 117: Cassowary © Shutterstock/Sanit Fuangnakhon
Page 119: Cassowary © Shutterstock/Bildagentur Zoonar GmbH

WOMBAT IN A BEANIE: All photographs © Alison Lester and Eddy Hume

ACKNOWLEDGEMENTS

Affirm Press wishes to thank everyone who willingly donated photographs to this collection of amazing animal stories, especially the Australian Reptile Park in New South Wales for the cover image of Kenny the wombat.

Thanks to Australian Reptile Park and Devil Ark, WIRES Northern Rivers, Wildlife Habitat in Port Douglas, IFAW, Parks Australia, Melbourne Museum, Phillip Island Nature Parks, Ballarat Wildlife Park, The Ark Animal Hospital Northern Territory, Australian Volunteer Coast Guard Association in Portland, the University of Adelaide, Main Roads Pilbara, Waroona Veterinary Clinic, and Debra Scott from Outback Pics for the generous donation of images. Special thanks to Amanda Woodbine, Sue Ulyatt, Naomi Will, Ashley Stewart, Helen Coutts, Clare Anderson, Narelle Spencer, Roland Pick, Mandy Hall, Stephen Brown, Rebekka Thompson-Jones and Vivienne Sykes for your time, patience and efforts locating the photographs for this book. We have also accessed images via Flickr and Wikimedia Commons, and we are extremely appreciative of photographers who release their images to the public domain.

Thanks to Hannah White and Amelia Mouradian for their research and contributions.